LITTLE BOOK OF REVISION
A Checklist for Fiction Writers

By Denise M. Baran-Unland for WriteOn Joliet

Cover by Rebekah Baran

This book is lovingly dedicated to the writer,
whoever you might be.

"One should not aim at being possible to understand, but at being impossible to misunderstand."
– Quintilian (Marcus Fabius Quintilianus, 1st century AD)

TABLE OF CONTENTS

INTRODUCTION

Like many people, I had a novel living in my head for a long time for I actually wrote it.

Like many people, or perhaps far more arrogantly than many people, I felt writing that novel, once I finally attempted, it nearly three decades later, would be, if not easy, then not too difficult.

By that time, I had spent nearly a decade contributing a decent income to my family as a freelance writer of features stories for newspapers and organizations.

I was a good features writer. But I didn't know beans about writing novels. And it showed in my pitiful drafts.

But by 2008, when I finally began writing my vampire novel in earnest, the internet was full of help. I cleaved to search engines in search of answers like my Victorian vampire clung to his victims.

I made notes about the most helpful advice, notes I'm sharing with you today in workbook form.

By placing one item to consider at a time, you can jot a few lines about what you did well, where trouble spots exist, and ideas for revision.

The book is intended to be your personal handbook for writing the best story you intended to write.

I've only provided some tidbits to feed your revision muse.

TYPES OF EDITING:

Beta reader: A person that reads your work and provides feedback.

Manuscript assessment: Wide critique of the manuscript's strengths and weaknesses, along with overall suggestions for improvement.

Development editing: Target content and structure: plot, pacing, dialogue, characterization, inconsistencies, wordiness, underwriting, and overwriting.

Line editing: Examines the manuscript line by line. Paragraphs may be rearranged, and Sentences may be written to ensure smooth Transitions and prose.

Copy editing: Corrects word choices, spelling, punctuation, and grammar.

Proofreading: Catches and corrects typos and minor errors in spelling, punctuation, and grammar.

BEFORE YOU START

1) Don't try to write a first draft perfect. You won't.

2) Getting the story out of your head and onto paper (or into the computer) is nothing more than dumping the wooden blocks on the floor and sorting them into piles so the real building can begin. Likewise, writing a first draft moves you to the place where the real writing can begin.

3) Once you have a draft, set it aside. This will give you distance from said draft, so you can evaluate it with ruthless objectivity when you return to it

4) Train yourself to discern the difference begin good writing, good enough writing, and writing that needs rewriting.

5) "Killing Your Darlings" doesn't mean killing every good combination of words. See number three.

6) Vary sentences, paragraphs, and chapters in terms of length, mood, and pacing.

7) Write sentences, paragraphs, and chapters the way you would tell a joke. Save the punch line for the end.

8) In the case of sentences and chapters, the punch line is the most words or information with the biggest punch, thrust, or bang. (See what I did here?).

9) Be wary of friends and family who love your work. They may love you more and (a) not be objective enough to give helpful feedback or (b) love you more than the work and be hesitant to tell you so.

10) Laugh a lot.

PLOT

Plot is the cause-and-effect sequence of events that form the structure of any story.

1) Are there any inconsistences or gaps in the plot?

2) Does the plot stay tight and interesting throughout the entire story, or does it sag (fall apart or become boring) in anyplace?

3) Is the plot believable?

4) Does the story stay focused on the plot?

5) Does the story start at the right place?

6) Is back story added in the appropriate places/times/amounts?

7) Check for areas where back story slows down the story.

8) Does the story progress in a logical (not necessarily linear) manner?

9) What about subplots? Too many? not enough?

10) Do surprises relate to the plot?

11) Is the climax strong and worth it to the reader?

12) Does the ending satisfy or disappoint?

13) Make sure the ending isn't abrupt and doesn't drag.

CHARACTERS

Characters are the people, places, animals, and objects in the story.

1) Are the main characters interesting and fully developed.

2) Do they have strengths and weaknesses? Quirks, habits, and interests?

3) Do they have clear goals and dreams?

3) Are they motivated in ways appropriate to the plot as well as their personalities and goals?

4) Are all characters vital to the story? Cut or combine those that don't contribute to the story in meaningful ways.

5) Do you have enough characters? Too many characters?

6) Do the characters grow with the story? If not, give them plot-appropriate challenges.

7) Are the characters appropriate to target reader age, era, and genre?

8) Are the characters believable?

9) Make sure response/actions/reactions are appropriate to the characters.

10) Do characters show appropriate emotion at the appropriate times?

DIALOGUE

Dialogue is the internal and external speech of the characters.

1) Does dialogue advance the plot, convey information increases conflict or tension, or mislead? (Yes, characters can lie).

2) Is dialogue true to characters, scenes, and interests?

3) Do characters sound distinct? This is especially important when several characters are similar in age, personality, and interest. Tip: Emphasize their differences in their speech patterns.

4) Is the dialogue age appropriate, gender appropriate, and person to person appropriate? For instance, a ten-year-old boy might speak differently to his teacher, his best friend, the school bully, his mother, and his dog.

5) Remember: the goal of dialogue is to SOUND natural, not BE natural. Much real-life conversation is boring and superfluous. Cut unnecessary dialogue from your manuscript.

6) Watch dialogue tags. Forget what your fifth grade English teacher said about mixing them up. "Said" is appropriate most of the time as it is the tag most likely to fade from readers' consciousness. Occasionally, other tags might be appropriate, especially when used as verbs. Use it AFTER the name of the person speaking. It will fade from the reader's mind.

7) Use even "said" sparingly. Enliven dialogue with bits of action, pauses, facial expressions, etc. to enliven the scene.

8) Create such distinct dialogue for your characters that readers can follow the voices without identifying them with tags.

9) Watch adverbs in tags. They're like curry. A little is nice, but too much overpowers the dialogue. You don't want your novel to sound like a Tom Swifty.

SCENES And CHAPTERS

A scene is a continuous event. A chapter holds one or more scenes and gives structure to the story. Good scenes and chapters have similar considerations.

1) Make sure to balance show and tell in scenes and chapters.

2) Does each chapter have a sufficient amount of conflict?

3) Does each scene/chapter serve a purpose?

4) Do the scenes/chapters have variety?

5) Do the scenes/chapters move the story forward?

6) Do scenes/chapters happen in the logical order to create tension and interest?

POINT OF VIEW

POV determines who is narrating the story, one or more characters or the writer.

1) Consider the different types of POV: all-knowing universal narrator, first person, second person, third person, third person perfect, unreliable narrator. What makes this best POV for this story or scene?

2) Is the POV maintained throughout the story or scene?

3) Is there head-hopping (telling the story from the point of views from different characters at the same time? Is it confusing to the reader, or does it add clarity?

4) Double-check characters so that they know what they should know and don't know what they should not.

PACING

Pace determines how fast or slow
the story moves.

1) Overall, does pace vary? Too slow, and the reader becomes bored. Too fast, and the reader can't absorb information.

2) Is the pace appropriate for each scene and chapter?

3) Do scenes/chapters have sufficient conflict to keep the story taut?

4) Is there sufficient conflict between characters?

5) Does tension escalate as the story progresses?

DEADWOOD

These are words and phrases that
dilute or choke off your story.
Consider them as weeds to your
garden.

All of the words here have appropriate uses, especially in dialogue.

However, all/most of them are some of the most overused words in manuscripts.

When revising your writing, watch for their overuse and cut and/or replace where necessary.

- Pronouns: he, she, it, you, they, we, him, her, etc.
- Forms of be: is, are, was, where
- Have, has, had, and especially "had had."
- There was.
- Almost any sentence that begins with the word "there."
- Just
- Still
- Now
- Very
- Only
- While
- So
- Up
- Down
- In
- Out
- Finally
- Really
- And, but
- Some
- Suddenly

- Either, though, however (especially at the end of a sentence).
- Own
- Felt
- Thought
- A lot
- Ever
- Never
- Too
- All
- Already
- Anyway
- Got
- Deep inside
- Sat down (the only way to sit is down).
- Stand up
- Such a
- Kind of
- Soft of
- Pretty (as in "a pretty good day")
- Whole other
- Adverb plus a very when one strong very can do the job
- Several adjectives in a row to create description
- Deep inside

Verbs: Use one precise verb to replace a weaker verb and adverbs. Example: Instead of "ran very quickly" say "sprinted" or "raced." Instead of "super happy" say "ecstatic."

Intensity: Beware of verbs that are too intense or not intense enough. If verbs are too intense, a simple scene can seem like life or death. Conversely, a life or death scene can become "meh" if the verb is not intense enough. And too much intensity too often can cause the reader to tune out the story.

Adverbs: Use to modify verbs, adjectives, and other adverbs when absolutely needed thoughts.

Adjectives: Used sparingly, they make people, places, animals, and objects vivid in the readers' mind. Too many in a row, and they cloud the image.

LEFTOVERS

These are miscellaneous considerations for revision that didn't belong anywhere else in this book.

1) Learn to spot "writer tics." All writers have them. These are certain writing patterns that come naturally to you and are used over and again.

2) Check each scene for use of the five senses. See if they need more or less of seeing, hearing, smelling, feeling, and//or tasting.

3) Check consistency in details for characters and settings.

4) Check facts and technicalities. An experienced archer will catch errors in archery scenes.

5) Use active (not passive verbs) as much as possible.

6) Recheck for any unnecessary forms of be, adjectives, adverbs, filtering, and deadwood.

7) Remove cliches, unless in dialogue and inherent to the character's speaking voice.

8) Check again for variances in sentence structure, length, and rhythm.

9) Word use should be consistent with character, era, and genre.

10) Rewrite overused words and phrases.

11) Use a dictionary to double-check meanings of words.

12) Check the timeline of your story's events.

FINALLY...

1) Read your story aloud. You'll catch errors and clumsy writing.

2) Read it backwards, same reasons.

3) Congratulate yourself and bask in your accomplishment! It's not everyone that can construct a new reality with letters and words.

ABOUT WRITEON JOLIET

WriteOn started as WriteOn Minooka, co-founded by Denise M. Baran-Unland and Kristina Skaggs. Our members
come from all over the southern suburbs.

Some have self-published or have been traditionally published. Others are still exploring their writing options and interests. Regardless of our place in the writing world, WriteOn welcomes everyone looking to write, read and grow.

WriteOn Joliet is a welcoming, diverse group of writers of varied skills, interests and experience. The group includes professional journalists, fiction novelists, bloggers, screenwriters, musicians and poets.

We promise a safe, comfortable and supportive atmosphere to share your work, and constructive
feedback so that everyone can benefit from our shared knowledge.

WriteOn is a dues-paying organization. The first visit is free.

WriteOn Joliet is a proud partner of the Joliet Public Library and The Book Market in Crest Hill.

For more information, visit writeonjoliet.com

ABOUT DENISE M. BARAN-UNLAND

Denise M. Baran-Unland is the author of the phantasmic BryonySeries. This includes the "drop of blood" vampire trilogy for young and new adults, Gothic prequel for adults, the Adventures of Cornell Dyer chapter book series for grade school children and the Bertrand the Mouse series for young children.

She has six adult children, three adult stepchildren, fourteen total grandchildren,
 six godchildren, and four cats.

She is the co-founder of WriteOn Joliet and previously taught features writing for a homeschool coop, with the students' work published in the co-op magazine and The Herald-News in Joliet.

Denise blogs daily and is currently the features editor at The Herald-News. To read her feature stories, vtheherald-news.com.

For more information about Denise's fiction and to follow her on social media,
visit bryonyseries.com.

ABOUT REBEKAH BARAN

Rebekah Baran is a pastry chef who also assists writers in their self-publishing journey by helping to format their books for print and web, design their websites, and guiding them through the general process.

Email her purpleroses33@gmail.com

www.ingramcontent.com/pod-product-compliance
Lightning Source LLC
Chambersburg PA
CBHW022126280326
41933CB00007B/561